# TIMOTHY

# TIMOTHY
## A Young Disciple

BOOK 3 OF THE Young yet Chosen! SERIES

Mrs. Stephanie Miller–Henderson, M.A., M.S.

XULON PRESS

Xulon Press
2301 Lucien Way #415
Maitland, FL 32751
407.339.4217
www.xulonpress.com

Unless otherwise indicated, Scripture quotations taken from the Africa Study Bible. (2012). Oasis International Limited.

Paperback ISBN-13: 978-1-6322-1842-1

# Dedication:

*To my husband, for your consistent love and support; my daughter, for being the best part of me; and my family, especially my sister, for always having my back.*

# Text Parts

## Main Characters:

Timothy-*teacher, evangelist*

Paul-*apostle, missionary*

Silas-*church leader, missionary*

Eunice-*Timothy's mother*

Lois-*Timothy's grandmother*

## Setting:

Second Missionary Journey; Derbe and Lystra

# Vocabulary Connection:

*Christian race*: unlike a competition with others, this is a figurative marathon where the runner is competing with him or herself, with comparison only to Jesus Christ.

*Faith:* reliance, loyalty or complete trust in God; a system of religious beliefs.

*Power:* ability to act or produce an effect; possession of control, authority, or influence over others; physical might; mental or moral efficacy.

*Missionary:* a strong purpose (especially of God); the task of bringing the Gospel to people from a different culture; people who bring the Gospel to other cultures.

*Gift:* a present from people to people; a sacrifice from people to God; anything given voluntarily or at no cost; that which is given from God, enabling or empowering His people.

*Scripture*: the law; the writings of Moses; the entire collection of sacred books.

*Salvation:* deliverance from the power and effects of sin, danger or difficulty by God's intervention.

**Vocabulary Reference:** African Study Bible. (2012). Oasis International Limited.

# Suggested Reading:

Acts 16:1-17:14
1 Timothy, II Timothy

Timothy's mother, Eunice,
taught him the Scriptures as a boy.

With his grandmother Lois
setting the same example,
Timothy's faith and heritage
would bring Paul and the Lord so much joy.

As a highly thought-of youth in the faith,
Timothy was able to accompany Paul
on his second missionary journey
where he would serve.

Timothy helped establish churches
at Philippi, Thessalonica, and Berea,
telling them about a man who
could save all humanity
and how our honor He deserved.

Paul sent for Timothy and Silas,
and Timothy was sent to Thessalonica
to strengthen the faith of believers there.

A trustworthy friend,
Timothy carried money collected
by the Philippian church for Paul's care.

Timothy was in Ephesus with Paul,
as he taught on God's amazing power.

Timothy had learned for years
how to teach and empower.

Paul thought highly of Timothy
and called him, his "son in the faith."

During his imprisonment,
Paul wrote two letters to Timothy
to encourage him in the Christian race.

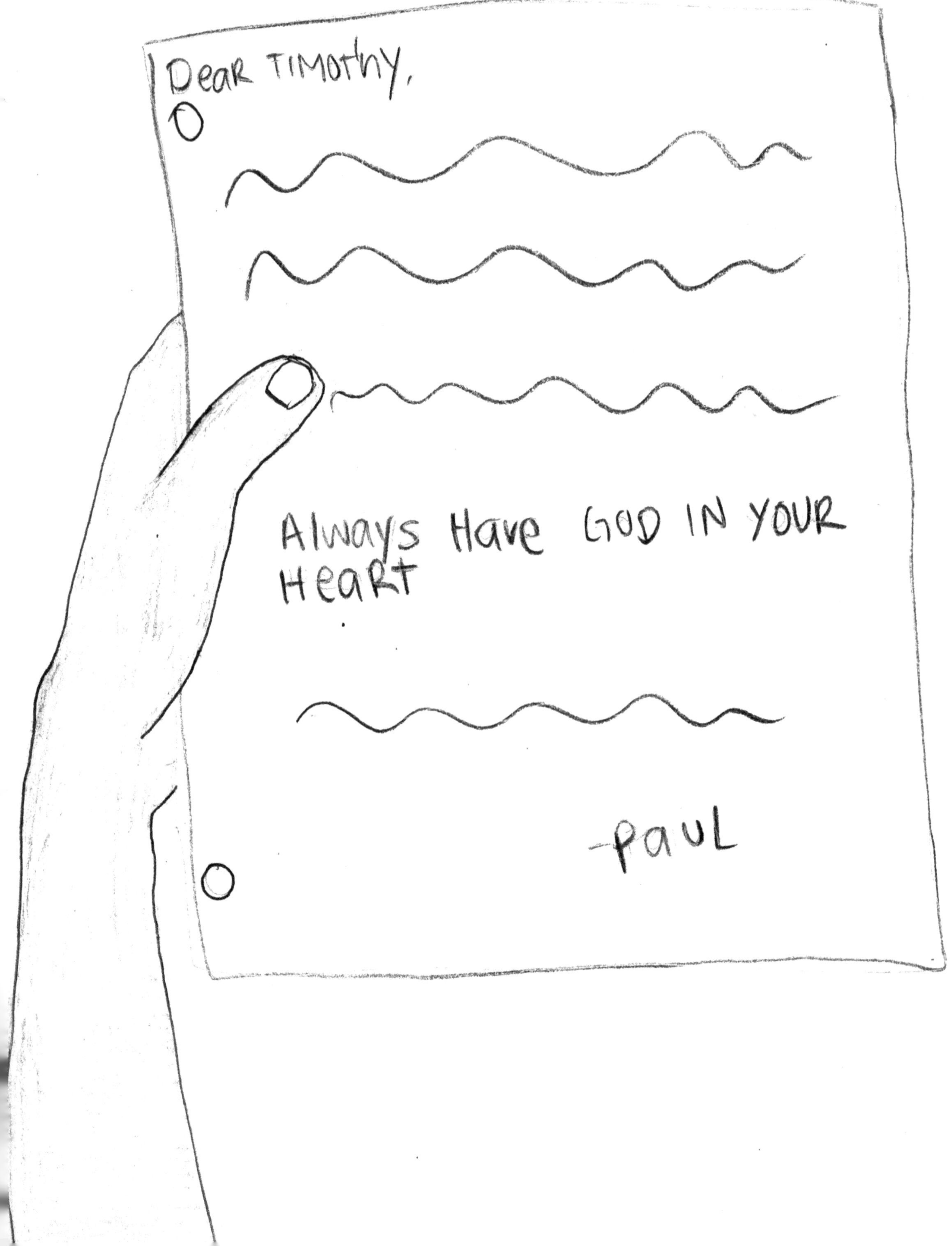
Dear TIMOTHY,
Always Have GOD IN YOUR HeaRT
-PAUL

In the first letter to Timothy,
Paul gave instructions and advice
for leading the church.

Paul told Timothy to be devoted to scripture
and not neglect the gift
God gave him on this earth.

Dear TIMOTHY

Be MINDFUL of People preaching
a FALSE Faith.

—PAUL

In the second letter,
Paul warned Timothy about false teachers
and to continue in the things he had learned.

Timothy had role models
in Paul, his mother, and grandmother,
and from those lessons in character,
he would not turn.

Timothy was made wise about salvation
from truths he learned as a young boy.

Like Timothy, we must stand firmly on God's truth,
presenting ourselves to God as one approved,
bringing Him eternal joy.

# R & R: Review & Reflect

1. Where was Timothy from?

2. How many letters did Paul write to Timothy?

# Read Further & Connect

3. How was Lydia's heart opened?

4. What example is Paul asking Timothy to set in *1 Timothy 4:12*?

5. According to *II Timothy 3:16*, how can all scripture be considered?

# ABOUT THE AUTHOR:

## Mrs. Stephanie Miller-Henderson, M.A., M.S.

# Biography

**Stephanie Miller-Henderson** is a southeast side of Chicago native who currently serves as an educator/counselor with the Chicago Public School district. Her previous professional experience includes 13 years in the social service field in the area of mental health where she also served as treatment team coordinator. Stephanie serves in several ministry capacities as a member of Calvary Baptist Church in Chicago where she is able to teach within the Sunday School department, serve as ministry leader for the Children of the King dance ministry, participate in various homeless outreach endeavors through the SEED ministry, fellowship with women of God in the women's ministry and coordinate several annual youth events through the youth ministry. With a passion in theatre, Stephanie also serves with the Drama Ministry. Stephanie has and continues to engage in Board service furthering her work and love for the Arts and increasing youth interest in the Sciences, Technology, Engineering, Arts and Math career pathways. Stephanie had the opportunity to travel to Nairobi and Mombasa, Kenya in 2016 where her daughter helped to facilitate arts programming for girls from 3 schools in the region. This helped to spark a desire to continue to work in the region which Stephanie will be able to do through Mommy and Me Ministries, Inc., an organization aiming to provide services for youth who have an incarcerated mother, in which she serves as founder and director. As a mother, the oldest of 7 siblings, an author and business owner, Stephanie understands the significance of providing resources, skills, encouragement and advocacy to youth throughout the city of Chicago and abroad. Introducing young people to the love of God is the foundation of it all!

# Acknowledgements:

A special thank-you to my pastor, Rev. Dr. James R. Flint Jr.,

and Calvary Baptist Church of Chicago's Christian education

department!

# About The Illustrator

**Aniyah Marie-Roze Harris** is a student at the
Chicago High School for the Arts (ChiArts).

CPSIA information can be obtained
at www.ICGtesting.com
Printed in the USA
LVHW021500121220
673925LV00005B/438